I DO HEREBY DARE

_____

(NAME)

TO BE A MAN OF GOD

_____

(SIGNED)

_____

(DATE)

This prayer journal is a companion to
Dare to Be a Man of God
Bible study devotional for men.
To order, visit www.MoreThanAConquerorBooks.com.

LORD, HELP ME DRAW NEAR TO YOU LIKE NEVER BEFORE. GIVE ME A PASSION FOR YOU SO STRONG I'LL NEVER TURN AWAY. I WANT TO SEE THROUGH YOUR EYES, FEEL WITH YOUR HEART, MAKE DECISIONS THROUGH YOUR WISDOM, LOVE THROUGH YOUR LOVE.

SO OFTEN, I DON'T FEEL WORTHY OR CAPABLE OF DOING THE THINGS I KNOW YOU'RE CALLING ME TO DO, BUT YOU, O LORD, ARE ALL-POWERFUL AND I CAN DO ALL THINGS THROUGH YOUR STRENGTH.

SO PLEASE TEACH ME TO LAY DOWN ALL MY AGENDAS, IDEAS, PLANS AND DREAMS, AND TAKE ON ONLY YOURS.

I WANT TO FEEL THE POWER OF YOUR LOVE AND BE MORE THAN A CONQUEROR IN EVERY BATTLE. TEACH ME TO WALK AS ONE WITH YOU AND IN THE EMPOWERING OF YOUR SPIRIT. DON'T LET ME LEAN ON MY OWN UNDERSTANDING ANYMORE, BUT TEACH ME TO TRUST IN YOU AS YOU LEAD ME IN THE PATHS YOU HAVE FOR ME.

AS I STUDY THROUGH YOUR WORD THIS YEAR, OPEN THE EYES OF MY HEART, TOPPLE EVERY STRONGHOLD THAT SETS ITSELF UP AGAINST THE KNOWLEDGE OF YOU, AND DESTROY EVERY LIE I BELIEVE. TEACH ME TO WALK IN YOUR TRUTH, FOR ONLY THE TRUTH CAN SET ME FREE.

SURROUND ME WITH YOUR FELT PRESENCE CONSTANTLY SO I'LL NEVER FORGET I'M IN THE PRESENCE OF SOMEONE HOLIER THAN I. TEAR DOWN MY PRIDE AND GIVE ME COURAGE TO WALK IN HUMILITY AND SURRENDER TO YOU EVERY DAY OF MY LIFE.

I ASK YOU FOR THE BIG THINGS THIS YEAR, LORD, FOR MIGHTY MIRACLES HAPPENING IN ME AND ALL AROUND ME LIKE NEVER BEFORE. MAKE ME A PURE VESSEL USEFUL TO BE USED FOR YOUR GLORY.

I LOVE YOU. TEACH ME TO LOVE YOU MORE.

SURRENDERING TO GOD IS TO YOUR ADVANTAGE.

NO MATTER HOW HARD YOU RUN AFTER THE THINGS YOU WANT
OR NEED IN LIFE, THEY WILL NEVER SATISFY YOU.
ONLY A DEEP, INTIMATE RELATIONSHIP WITH CHRIST WILL.

x

NO ONE GETS EVERYTHING HE WANTS IN THIS LIFE, EXCEPT THE MAN WHOSE
DESIRE IS FOR GOD. THEN GOD WILL MOST CERTAINLY SATISFY HIM WITH
HIMSELF.

LOOK FOR WHAT GOD HAS FOR YOU INSTEAD OF WHAT YOU THINK YOU
WANT, AND YOU WILL FIND HE IS ALL YOU NEED.

LIST THE THINGS YOU WANT MOST IN LIFE (LIKE A BEAUTIFUL WIFE, A GREAT CAREER, ETC.). PICTURE YOURSELF BOWING BEFORE JESUS' THRONE, AND THEN LAY EACH ONE OF THOSE THINGS YOU DESIRE AT HIS FEET.

_____

_____

_____

_____

_____

_____

_____

_____

_____

_____

_____

_____

_____

_____

_____

_____

_____

_____

_____

_____

_____

_____

_____

_____

NOW LAY YOURSELF AT JESUS' FEET. WRITE HIM A PRAYER OF SURRENDER.

GOD WILL MAKE SOMETHING BEAUTIFUL FROM YOUR MESSES, IF YOU LET HIM.

GOD ALREADY HAS A PERFECT PLAN FOR YOUR LIFE. THE SOVEREIGN ONE
WHO CREATED YOU, WHO LOVES YOU WITH NO BOUNDARIES, HAS ALREADY
PLANNED FOR YOU THE BEST ... HIMSELF!

THE GOD WHO LOVES YOU IS IN CONTROL. HE HAS A PLAN, AND IT'S A GOOD ONE.
ROMANS 8:28. HE LOVES YOU. AND THAT'S A PEACEFUL PLACE TO REST.

IS ANYTHING YOU'RE REACHING FOR TAKING YOU OFF-TRACK?

NOTICE WHAT DISTRACTS YOU, HAND THOSE THOUGHTS TO JESUS,
ASK HIM FOR HIS, AND GET BACK ON TRACK.

HAND EVERYTHING OVER TO GOD AND REST IN HIS SOVEREIGNTY. ISAIAH 30:15. SURRENDER TO HIM, KNOWING YOU CAN TRUST HIM, EVEN IF THE OUTCOME ISN'T WHAT YOU EXPECT. WHATEVER GOD IS DOING, IT IS GOOD BECAUSE *HE* IS GOOD.

THIS WHOLE RACE IS ABOUT RELATIONSHIP, NOT WORKS. SO, DON'T JUST TRY
TO WILL YOURSELF TO DO THE RIGHT THING, ALTHOUGH YOUR WILL TO FOL-
LOW CHRIST IS MOST CERTAINLY CRUCIAL. IT'S JUST NOT ENOUGH. YOU NEED
SOMEONE STRONGER. SEEK TO FALL DEEPER IN LOVE WITH JESUS. THEN HIS
LOVE IN YOU AND YOUR PASSION FOR HIM WILL FUEL YOUR WILL TO COME
IN LINE WITH HIS. ROMANS 8:35-39.

ARE ANY WRONG THOUGHT PROCESSES WEIGHING YOU DOWN OR KEEPING
YOU FROM FIXING YOUR EYES ON JESUS AND RUNNING WELL?

IF YOU COULD PICTURE THE THOUGHT-BURDENS YOU'VE CARRYING AS AN
OBJECT WEIGHING YOU DOWN, WHAT WOULD THAT BE?

PICTURE YOURSELF HANDING YOUR BURDENS TO JESUS ONE BY ONE. WHAT IS
HE GIVING YOU IN RETURN? ASK HIM TO SHOW YOU. ... RECEIVE IT.

A FEW OF THE WAYS GOD SPEAKS:

† HIS WORD (2 TIMOTHY 3:16-17)
† CIRCUMSTANCES (2 CORINTHIANS 12:7-10; PSALM 40:1-3)
† OTHERS (1 CORINTHIANS 2:4-13)
† HIS STILL SMALL VOICE IN OUR MIND, HEART (JOHN 14:26, EZEKIAL 18:1)
† DREAMS AND VISIONS (ACTS 2:17)
† IMPRESSIONS OR URGINGS (ACTS 15:28)
† A SENSE OF PEACE (PHILIPPIANS 4:7)
† SIGNS AND WONDERS (ACTS 2:17-21)
† NATURE (PSALM 125; 19:1-4)

IF YOU FEEL YOU CAN'T "HEAR" GOD YET, DON'T LET IT WORRY YOU. JUST
KEEP ASKING HIM QUESTIONS AND LOOKING FOR HIS ANSWERS. HE MAY NOT
ANSWER THE WAY YOU EXPECT, BUT IF YOU'RE SURRENDERED TO HIM, HE
WON'T LET YOU MISS HIS WILL.

EVERYONE MAKES MISTAKES. BUT THE MAN WHO FIXES HIS EYES ON JESUS
GROWS THROUGH HIS MISTAKES AND RUNS FASTER.

MOST PEOPLE RECEIVE THEIR IDENTITY THROUGH WHAT THEY DO, BUT YOUR
IDENTITY IS FOUND IN WHAT CHRIST HAS DONE FOR YOU.

THE WORLD MAKES DECISIONS BASED ON WHAT OTHERS EXPECT OF THEM,
WHAT SEEMS BEST, PERSONAL GAIN, FEAR, LOW SELF-ESTEEM, OR ANY
NUMBER OF OTHER THOUGHTS, URGES, OR EMOTIONS. BUT YOU ARE A
PRINCE, HEIR TO THE KINGDOM. YOU MAKE DECISIONS BASED ON YOUR
KING'S LORDSHIP OVER YOUR LIFE.

HEAVEN IS YOUR HOME NOW, AND YOUR CULTURE IS KINGDOM OF GOD
CULTURE. THAT MEANS YOU DO THINGS THE WAY JESUS DOES, NOT THE WAY
OTHERS THINK YOU SHOULD.

ONLY GOD'S OPINION MATTERS. YOU ARE WHO HE SAYS YOU ARE, NOT WHAT
OTHERS SAY OR THINK ABOUT YOU.

WALK OUT IN THE TRUTH OF WHO YOU ARE IN CHRIST. IF YOU'RE HIS
FRIEND, THEN TALK WITH HIM, HANG OUT WITH HIM, KNOW HE'S WITH YOU
EVERYWHERE YOU GO AND THAT HE'S FOR YOU. IF YOU'RE GOD'S SON, THEN
TAKE ON HIS CHARACTER IN THE WAY YOU SPEAK AND ACT.

EVERYTHING WE BELIEVE AND THINK MUST AGREE WITH WHAT GOD SAYS OR
WE COULD BE LISTENING TO A DIFFERENT FATHER—THE FATHER OF LIES.
JOHN 8:42-47.

THAT HOLE IN YOUR HEART THAT LONGS FOR THE PERFECT FATHER IS GOD-
SIZED. RELEASE YOUR FATHER TO NOT BE GOD AND GOD TO BE YOUR FATHER.

"DRAW NEAR TO GOD, AND HE WILL DRAW NEAR TO YOU." JAMES 4:8.

34

LET JESUS BE YOUR FIRST THOUGHT WHEN YOU WAKE, YOUR LAST THOUGHT
AS YOU SLEEP, AND ALL YOUR THOUGHTS IN BETWEEN.

HAND JESUS EVERY DAY BEFORE IT EVEN STARTS AND LOOK FOR HIM ALL
THROUGHOUT THE DAY. SHARE WITH HIM YOUR THOUGHTS
AND LISTEN FOR HIS ANSWERS.

THE CLOSER YOU WALK WITH CHRIST, THE MORE ABUNDANT AND
MEANINGFUL YOUR LIFE WILL BE. JOHN 10:10B.

37

THE ENEMY'S MAIN AIM IS TO STOP YOU FROM PRAYING.

YOU WERE CREATED TO MAKE A DIFFERENCE IN THIS WORLD. BUT IF YOU
STRIVE IN YOUR OWN STRENGTH, YOU'LL WEAR YOURSELF OUT.

PLAN A TIME THIS MONTH TO SPEND HALF A DAY ALONE WITH GOD.

THE SECRET PLACE IS WHERE YOU REST FROM THE BATTLE. WHERE YOU
COMMUNE WITH YOUR HEAVENLY FATHER. WHERE HE TEACHES YOU AND
TRAINS YOU TO GET READY FOR THE DIFFICULTIES THAT LIE AHEAD. WHERE
HE EMPOWERS YOU TO CONQUER THE ENEMY. AND IT'S ALSO WHERE YOU
LEARN TO FLY. DEUTERONOMY 32:11-12.

THROUGHOUT THE DAY, PRAY AND LISTEN FOR GOD'S LEADING BEFORE MAKING DECISIONS, WHETHER BIG OR SMALL. IF YOU DON'T, YOU MAY MISS THE MIRACLE!

ANYTHING GOD DOES OR ASKS YOU TO DO WILL ALWAYS AGREE WITH HIS WORD, NOT JUST A TINY PORTION OF IT, BUT ALL OF IT. ONE POWERFUL WAY, THEN, TO PARTNER WITH GOD IN AGREEING WITH HIS PURPOSES AND CALLING THEM FORTH INTO THE WORLD AROUND YOU IS TO PRAY SCRIPTURE.

LOOK FOR WHAT GOD'S DOING AND JOIN HIM THERE.

LOOK FOR WHAT GOD'S DOING AND JOIN HIM THERE.

GOD IS GOD, AND HE CAN DO ANYTHING HE WANTS ANY TIME. BUT HE MOST
OFTEN WAITS FOR US TO PRAY BEFORE HE ACTS. HE DOESN'T JUST WANT TO
GET SOMETHING DONE; HE WANTS TO DO SOMETHING WITH US AND IN US.

GOD IS ALWAYS DOING SOMETHING AMAZING. PRAYER GIVES YOU A FRONT-
ROW SEAT AND POSITIONS YOU TO BE USED BY HIM.

WORSHIP ISN'T JUST SOMETHING WE DO ON SUNDAYS. IT IS A LIFESTYLE.

48

WORSHIPPING GOD TRANSFORMS BOTH YOU AND WHAT YOU'RE GOING
THROUGH.

IF EVER YOU HAVE A BAD DREAM OR WAKE UP IN A PANIC, TELL THE ENEMY
TO FLEE, AND THEN WORSHIP THE LORD. WORSHIP INVITES GOD NEAR AND
MAKES THE ENEMY TREMBLE.

GOD SOMETIMES MEETS US IN OBVIOUS WAYS. BUT MORE OFTEN, HIS TOUCH IS
SO SOFT WE MUST DRAW NEAR TO HIM TO FEEL IT. JAMES 4:8A.

GOD IS SPEAKING ALL THE TIME. IF YOU THINK YOU CAN'T HEAR HIM, LOOK FOR SIN OR WRONG THOUGHT PROCESSES BLOCKING YOUR SPIRITUAL "EARS."

IF YOU LISTEN TO FEAR OR DOUBT, YOU'LL MISS THE VOICE THAT COUNTS.

DO YOU FEEL DISTRACTED IN YOUR QUIET TIMES? PRAY, ASKING GOD
TO GUARD THAT TIME AND GUIDE IT. DON'T JUST STICK TO WHAT YOU
NORMALLY DO. ASK GOD WHAT HE WANTS TO DO AND FOLLOW HIM THERE.

DO YOUR THOUGHTS DART ABOUT, MAKING IT DIFFICULT TO FOCUS IN YOUR
QUIET TIMES? TURN THOSE THOUGHTS INTO PRAYERS. IS THERE SOME TASK
YOU NEED TO GET DONE THAT YOU CAN'T STOP THINKING ABOUT? KEEP A
NOTEPAD HANDY AND WRITE IT DOWN SO YOU DON'T FORGET,
AND THEN GO BACK TO LISTENING TO THE LORD.

HAVE YOU DECIDED ON THE LIE THAT GOD DOESN'T SPEAK,
OR THAT HE SPEAKS TO OTHERS BUT NOT TO YOU?
IF YOU EXPECT GOD TO SPEAK, YOU'RE MORE LIKELY TO HEAR HIM.

_____

_____

_____

_____

_____

_____

_____

_____

_____

_____

_____

_____

_____

_____

_____

_____

_____

_____

_____

_____

_____

_____

_____

_____

_____

WHAT IF YOU THINK YOU'RE HEARING GOD BUT YOU'RE NOT SURE?
ASK HIM, "LORD, ARE YOU SAYING ...?" IF YOU'RE STILL NOT SURE, HAND
WHAT YOU FEEL HIM SAYING BACK OVER TO HIM: "LORD, IT FEELS LIKE
YOU'RE SAYING.... I'M HEADED THAT WAY BECAUSE I WANT TO OBEY YOU.
PLEASE MAKE YOUR WILL CLEAR."

MAKE TIME IN EVERY QUIET TIME TO SIT STILL BEFORE THE LORD
AND LISTEN TO HIM.

DON'T DISMISS GOD'S VOICE WITH, "THAT'S JUST ME" OR "I'LL THINK ABOUT
THAT LATER." TUNING OUT GOD IS LIKE CLOSING THE DOOR IN HIS FACE.

THE KEY TO LISTENING IS OBEDIENCE. EACH TIME YOU STEP OUT IN FAITH TO DO WHAT GOD ASKS OF YOU, HIS VOICE GETS LOUDER AND OBEYING HIM GETS EASIER. BUT IF YOU IGNORE HIM, THERE MAY COME A TIME WHEN YOU CAN NO LONGER HEAR WHAT HE'S SAYING. ISAIAH 55:6.

THREE-FOLD SIEVE FOR KNOWING
GOD'S VOICE OF TRUTH:

1. DOES IT LINE UP WITH THE WORD
   (ALL OF IT, NOT JUST ONE VERSE)?

2. DOES IT LINE UP WITH GOD'S
   CHARACTER (ESPECIALLY HIS LOVE
   AND GRACE)? MATTHEW 22:37-40.

3. DOES IT DRAW YOU (AND OTHERS)
   CLOSER TO HIM?

HUMILITY IS AGREEING WITH GOD.

_____

HUMILITY IS FOCUSING YOUR EYES ON GOD, NOT YOURSELF.

HUMILITY IS SURRENDERING TO GOD.

HUMILITY DRAWS US INTO GOD'S PRESENCE AND PLACES US
IN THE RIGHT POSITION FOR INTIMACY WITH HIM.

HUMILITY IS ALWAYS BEING CONSCIOUS YOU ARE IN THE PRESENCE
OF ONE GREATER THAN YOU.

HUMILITY IS DEPENDING ON GOD.

THE EASIEST WAY TO BREAK FREE FROM A SIN STRONGHOLD IS TO SEE YOUR
SIN THE WAY GOD SEES IT, TO AGREE WITH HIM ABOUT IT.

_____
_____
_____
_____
_____
_____
_____
_____
_____
_____
_____
_____
_____
_____
_____
_____
_____
_____
_____
_____
_____
_____
_____
_____
_____
_____
_____
_____
_____
_____
_____
_____
_____

JUST BECAUSE YOU BELIEVE SOMETHING DOESN'T MEAN IT'S TRUE. ONLY WHAT
GOD SAYS IS TRUE. WHEN YOU DISAGREE WITH HIM, YOU SET YOURSELF ABOVE
HIM, AS IF YOU KNOW BETTER THAN GOD.

_____

_____

_____

_____

_____

_____

_____

_____

_____

_____

_____

_____

_____

_____

_____

_____

_____

_____

_____

_____

_____

_____

_____

_____

_____

_____

WHEN YOU LIVE IN FEAR OF THE LORD, YOU'RE MORE AFRAID
OF THE CONSEQUENCES OF NOT OBEYING GOD
THAN YOU ARE OF NOT GETTING WHAT YOU WANT.

TRUE OBEDIENCE FLOWS NATURALLY FROM A PASSIONATE LOVE FOR CHRIST.
THE CLOSER YOU WALK WITH JESUS, THE EASIER IT IS TO OBEY HIM.

THERE'S NO FASTER WAY TO ONENESS WITH CHRIST THAN SURRENDER.

LET THE TRUTH YOU KNOW BECOME THE TRUTH YOU LIVE.

A WISE MAN KNOWS HE CAN'T LEAN ON HIS OWN UNDERSTANDING, EVEN
IF HE HAS ALL THE "FACTS," BECAUSE MAN'S WISDOM ISN'T COMPLETE.

HOW TO MAKE WISE
DECISIONS:
1. LAY YOUR AGEN-
DAS DOWN.
2. ASK GOD WHAT HE
WANTS TO DO.
3. MAKE SURE YOU
KNOW THE FACTS.
NO MIND-READING
OR IMAGINING.
4. PRAY WITH THOSE
AFFECTED BY YOUR
DECISION.
5. HAND ANY ADVICE
OVER TO GOD.
6. MAKE SURE YOUR
DECISION AND THE
PATH TO GET THERE
ARE LOVING. MAT-
THEW 22:37-40.
7. "LORD, IT FEELS
LIKE YOU'RE
SAYING..., SO I'M
HEADED IN THAT
DIRECTION TO FOL-
LOW YOU. SHOW
ME CLEARLY IF I'M
WRONG."

WHAT ARE YOU FULL OF? THAT'S WHAT WILL COME OUT UNDER PRESSURE.

STEPS TO PEACE IN CONFLICT:
1. BE QUICK TO LISTEN, SLOW TO SPEAK, AND SLOW TO GET ANGRY. JAMES 1:19.
2. DON'T JUST REACT. LAY DOWN YOUR THOUGHTS AND ASK GOD FOR HIS. MARK 11:11-17; PROVERBS 3:5-7; ISAIAH 55:6-9.
3. GET ALONE AS SOON AS YOU CAN AND PRAY. USE THE GALATIANS 5:22-23 GAUGE IN CHAPTER 22.
4. CHECK FOR SIN. DID YOU HAVE A PART IN THE CONFLICT? MATTHEW 7:1-5.
5. IF SO, ASK FORGIVENESS. 1 JOHN 1:8-10.
6. NO MIND-READING. MAKE SURE YOU KNOW THE FACTS BEFORE YOU ACCUSE. ASK, "WHEN YOU SAID..., DID YOU MEAN...?" ONLY GOD KNOWS WHAT YOUR BROTHER IS THINKING AND ONLY HE IS THE JUDGE OF HIS MOTIVES. JAMES 4:11-12.
7. CHOOSE TO DO THE OPPOSITE OF WHAT THE ENEMY IS DOING.
8. ASK GOD WHAT HE'S DOING, SO YOU CAN COME IN LINE WITH HIS PURPOSES.
9. FORGIVE. MARK 11:25.

IN THE SPIRITUAL REALM, OUR ARMOR IS NOT JUST A METAPHOR. IT IS REAL.
THE ENEMY CAN SEE WHERE WE'RE VULNERABLE, AND THAT'S WHERE HE IS
MOST LIKELY TO STRIKE. SO BE ON THE ALERT. EPHESIANS 6:10-20.

YOU HAVE AN ENEMY, BUT IT'S NOT YOUR BROTHER. SO FIGHT FOR YOUR
BROTHER, NOT AGAINST HIM. EPHESIANS 6:10-28.

SATAN CAN'T ATTACK YOU UNLESS GOD ALLOWS IT. AND IF GOD ALLOWS IT,
THEN IT IS BECAUSE HE IS DOING SOMETHING GOOD IN YOU.

USE THE GALATIANS 5:22-23 GAUGE TO TEAR DOWN STRONGHOLDS SO YOU CAN WALK IN THE SPIRIT:

1. NOTICE WHEN YOU FEEL ANYTHING NEGATIVE OUTSIDE THE FRUIT OF THE SPIRIT.

2. EXCUSE YOURSELF FROM THE SITUATION AND GET ALONE WITH GOD.

3. ASK HIM WHY YOU FEEL THAT WAY. WHERE DID THAT FEELING, THOUGHT OR REACTION FIRST ENTER YOUR LIFE? LET HIM TAKE YOU ANYWHERE HE WANTS TO TAKE YOU AND SHOW YOU ANYTHING HE WANTS TO SHOW YOU.

4. IF HE BRINGS A MEMORY TO MIND, REMEMBER WHAT YOU FELT WHEN THAT HAPPENED. LOOK FOR THE LIES, LIKE, "I'M NOT GOOD ENOUGH," AND ANY VOWS LIKE, "I'LL NEVER LET ANYONE DO THAT TO ME AGAIN!"

5. NOW ASK GOD FOR HIS TRUTH. HE WAS THERE WHEN THAT HAPPENED. ASK HIM WHAT HE WAS SAYING AND DOING. (HE MIGHT REMIND YOU OF A VERSE, SPEAK LOVING WORDS TO YOU, OR SHOW YOU WHAT HE WAS DOING WHEN THAT HAPPENED.)

6. CANCEL ANY SELF-PROTECTIVE VOWS AND HAND YOUR LIFE BACK INTO GOD'S HANDS.

PRAYER FOR SHUTTING THE DOOR ON GENERATIONAL SINS:

"LORD, I FORGIVE _____ FOR OPENING THE DOOR TO SATAN WITH REGARD TO THE SIN OF _____.
PLEASE FORGIVE ME, LORD, FOR MY INVOLVEMENT IN THAT SIN. I DON'T WANT IT ANYMORE, AND I'M ASKING YOU TO EMPOWER ME NOW TO SHUT THE DOOR AND BEGIN A NEW TREND IN MY FAMILY LINE, ONE OF OBEDIENCE TO YOU ALONE. I RENOUNCE THAT GENERATIONAL SIN, AND IN THE NAME OF JESUS I CUT OFF ANY CURSES THAT MAY HAVE FALLEN ON ME OR MY FAMILY BECAUSE OF IT. I NOW COMMAND ANY DEMONS ("LUST," "ANGER," ETC.) TO GO TO THE FEET OF JESUS TO BE DEALT WITH BY HIM, AND I FORBID THE ENEMY TO EVER PICK ON ME, MY CHILDREN OR MY CHILDREN'S CHILDREN EVER AGAIN. I THANK YOU, LORD, THAT YOUR BLOOD HAS WASHED AWAY ALL MY SIN, AND THAT YOU COVER ME. PLEASE BE A SHIELD AROUND ME AND MY FAMILY, PROTECTING US FROM THE ENEMY'S SCHEMES. I ASK YOU NOW, LORD, TO FILL US WITH THE OPPOSITE THAT IS YOU (LOVE, FAITHFULNESS, PEACE, ETC) AND TO BLESS US WITH _____. PLEASE SET MY FAMILY MEMBERS AND ME FREE FROM THIS STRONGHOLD FOREVER. IN YOUR NAME, AMEN."

PRAY CLEANSING PRAYERS THROUGH YOUR HOME, ASKING GOD TO SEND
OUT ANYTHING UNCLEAN AND TO FILL YOUR HOME WITH HIS PRESENCE.
DEUTERONOMY 7.

IN EVERY SITUATION AND EVERY TRIAL, LOOK FOR WHAT GOD'S DOING AND
FOLLOW HIM THERE.

IF YOU'RE NOT SURE WHAT GOD'S DOING, AT LEAST
PURPOSE TO DO THE OPPOSITE OF WHAT THE ENEMY IS DOING.

YOU WERE CREATED FOR ONENESS, INTIMACY, LOVE, ACCEPTANCE, WORTH, BELONGING, POWER. BUT THOSE HOLES ARE GOD-SIZED. IF YOU TRY TO FILL THEM WITH LUST, PORNOGRAPHY, MASTURBATION, HOMOSEXUALITY OR OTHER SEXUAL ACTS, YOU WILL COME UP EMPTY.

THE MOST POWERFUL DETERRENT TO TEMPTATION IS
A DEEP, VIBRANT RELATIONSHIP WITH GOD.

IF YOU EXPERIENCE AN OVERWHELMING DRAW TO TURN YOUR HEAD AND THINK LUSTFUL THOUGHTS ABOUT A WOMAN, EITHER YOU OR SHE MAY HAVE A SEXUAL STRONGHOLD AND THE DEMONS ASSIGNED TO DRAW MEN TO THE THOUGHT OF HER COULD BE TUGGING AT YOU. EPHESIANS 6:12. TRY SAYING UNDER YOUR BREATH, "IF THIS IS THE ENEMY, STOP IT IN THE NAME OF JESUS!" THEN PRAY FOR HER FREEDOM, SALVATION, ETC. IF THE ENEMY SEES HE'S LOSING MORE GROUND BY TEMPTING YOU THAN IF HE LEAVES YOU ALONE, HE WILL LEAVE YOU ALONE!

LOOK AT EVERY WOMAN AS A SISTER OF CHRIST. TREAT HER WITH DIGNITY, RESPECT AND ABSOLUTE PURITY, AS JESUS WOULD.

87

THE WIFE GOD GIVES YOU WILL BE A PRECIOUS TREASURE. GUARD YOUR KISS-
ES AND YOUR BODY AS A WEDDING GIFT TO HER AND HER ALONE AS LONG
AS YOU BOTH LIVE. REMEMBER, SHE IS LOOKING FOR A GODLY MAN TOO.

DON'T LET SHAME AND SELF-CONDEMNATION OVERWHELM YOU. IF YOU
FALL, RECEIVE GOD'S FORGIVENESS, FORGIVE YOURSELF, LET GOD SHOW YOU
WHAT THOUGHTS LED YOU TO FALL SO YOU CAN LEARN AND GROW,
AND THEN GET UP AND WALK AGAIN!

YOUR FAITH MUST BE IN GOD HIMSELF, NOT IN CIRCUMSTANCES, OTHERS, YOURSELF, OR EVEN IN WHAT YOU WANT GOD TO DO.

THE KEY TO ASKING FOR SOMETHING IN JESUS' NAME IS TO WALK SO CLOSE
TO HIM THAT YOU KNOW HIS HEART AND WHAT HE'S DOING. JOHN 14:10-21.
THEN WHEN HE WANTS TO DO A MIRACLE, YOU WON'T MISS THE SHOW!

ASK GOD WHAT LIES YOU'RE BELIEVING THAT DISTANCE YOU FROM HIM.
WRITE THEM IN THE LEFT COLUMN. THEN ASK HIM FOR HIS TRUTH AND
WRITE IT IN THE RIGHT COLUMN:

LIES   TRUTH

_____

_____

_____

_____

_____

_____

_____

_____

_____

_____

_____

_____

_____

_____

_____

_____

_____

_____

_____

_____

_____

_____

_____

TO FIND THE LIES YOU REACT OUT OF INSTEAD OF THE HOLY SPIRIT, USE THE GALATIANS 5:22-23 GAUGE REGULARLY OR RUN YOUR THOUGHTS THROUGH THE THREE-FOLD SIEVE:

1. DOES IT AGREE WITH GOD'S WORD? (ALL OF IT, NOT JUST A PORTION)
2. DOES IT AGREE WITH GOD'S CHARACTER, ESPECIALLY LOVE AND GRACE?
3. DOES IT DRAW YOU CLOSER TO HIM?

WHAT DO YOU MOSTLY TALK ABOUT THESE DAYS?
THAT'S HOW YOU KNOW WHAT YOU'RE MOST PASSIONATE ABOUT.

LET THE NAME "JESUS" BE THE MOST COMMON WORD IN YOUR VOCABULARY.

SEEK TO LOVE MORE THAN TO BE LOVED,
TO UNDERSTAND MORE THAN TO BE UNDERSTOOD,
TO GIVE MORE THAN TO RECEIVE,
TO SERVE MORE THAN TO BE SERVED.

A POWERFUL KEY TO GROWING AND "FLOWING" IN CHRIST ALL YOUR LIFE
IS TO SURROUND YOURSELF WITH MATURE, GODLY PEOPLE WHO HAVE BEEN
THROUGH THE HARD THINGS AND HAVE COME OUT VICTORIOUS.

DON'T LEAN ON YOUR OWN UNDERSTANDING AS YOU MAKE DAILY
DECISIONS; WHETHER BIG OR SMALL. LOOK TO GOD.
ASK HIM WHAT HE WANTS TO DO AND FOLLOW HIM THERE.

IF YOU'RE LOVING GOD AND YOU'RE LOVING OTHERS, THEN YOU'RE DOING
EVERYTHING GOD HAS ASKED YOU TO DO! MATTHEW 22:37-40.

WE LOVE, NOT BECAUSE THE PERSON DESERVES IT, BUT BECAUSE CHRIST FIRST
LOVED US. 1 JOHN 4:19-21. WE FORGIVE, NOT BECAUSE WHAT THEY DID WAS
OKAY, BUT BECAUSE WE HAVE BEEN FORGIVEN.

THE BEST WAY TO MISS WHAT GOD'S DOING IN YOU
IS TO POINT YOUR FINGER AT SOMEONE ELSE.

FORGIVENESS IS RELEASING YOUR OFFENDER INTO THE HANDS OF GOD FOR
HIM TO DEAL WITH, AND RELEASING YOUR OWN HEART FROM THE CHAINS
THAT BIND YOU TO THE SIN DONE AGAINST YOU.

STEPS TO FREEDOM THROUGH FORGIVENESS:

1. BEFORE YOU JUDGE THE OTHER PERSON FOR WHAT HE DID WRONG, MAKE SURE THE SIN ISN'T ACTUALLY YOUR OWN. DID YOU DO SOMETHING TO INSTIGATE THE OTHER PERSON'S RESPONSE? ARE YOU ALSO IN SOME WAY GUILTY OF WHAT YOU'RE ACCUSING HIM OF? ARE YOU JUDGING OR MIND-READING (DECIDING WHAT HE'S THINKING OR WHAT MOTIVE HE HAD)? MATTHEW 7:1-5, JAMES 4:10-12. ONLY GOD KNOWS WHAT SOMEONE ELSE IS THINKING.

2. WHENEVER YOU FEEL ANGRY OR HURT, GO TO YOUR DIVINE COUNSELOR AND ASK HIM WHY YOU FEEL THAT WAY. ASK HIM WHEN WAS THE FIRST TIME THAT FEELING OR RESPONSE DEVELOPED IN YOUR LIFE, AND LET HIM TAKE YOU ANYWHERE HE WANTS TO TAKE YOU AND SHOW YOU ANY-THING HE WANTS TO SHOW YOU. HE MAY BRING BACK TO A CHILDHOOD MEMORY.

3. ALLOW YOURSELF TO REMEMBER THAT EVENT AND FEEL WHAT YOU FELT WHEN IT HAPPENED. LOOK FOR THE LIES (LIKE, "EVERYONE'S AGAINST ME. I HAVE TO DEFEND MYSELF.")

4. STILL IN THAT MEMORY, CHOOSE TO FORGIVE.
   - SAY, "I FORGIVE (NAME) FOR (OFFENSE)."
   - LAY DOWN ALL YOUR OPINIONS AND IDEAS ABOUT THAT PERSON AT JESUS' FEET AND ASK FOR HIS.
   - PRAY FOR HIM AND BLESS HIM.

5. IF YOU MADE A VOW (LIKE, "I'LL NEVER LET ANYONE DO THAT TO ME AGAIN!") BREAK IT.

6. ASK GOD FOR HIS TRUTH. "LORD, YOU WERE THERE WHEN THAT HAP-PENED. WHAT WERE YOU DOING AND SAYING?" RUN IT THROUGH THE THREE-FOLD SIEVE.

7. NOW FORGIVE THE OFFENDER IN YOUR CURRENT SITUATION. BLESS HIM. PRAY FOR HIM.

8. IF THE OFFENSE REPLAYS IN YOUR MIND, DON'T WORRY ABOUT IT, NO MATTER HOW MANY TIMES IT HAPPENS, JUST REMIND YOURSELF, "I FORGIVE ... AND I BLESS HIM IN JESUS' NAME," AND THEN PRAY FOR HIM AGAIN. IF YOU PRAY ALL THE MORE FOR OTHERS' SALVATION AND FREE-DOM WHEN SATAN ATTACKS YOU, EVENTUALLY HE'LL LEAVE YOU ALONE AND THAT OLD OFFENSE WON'T COME TO MIND ANYMORE.

FORGIVENESS IS A DECISION.
EVEN IF YOU DON'T "FEEL" LIKE FORGIVING, MAKE A CONSCIOUS CHOICE TO
FORGIVE ANYWAY, AND YOUR HEART WILL EVENTUALLY FOLLOW.

DON'T ASSESS A SITUATION BASED ON WHAT YOU THINK YOU DISCERN OR
EVEN YOUR OWN EXPERIENCE. ASK GOD HOW HE SEES IT.

DON'T ASSUME YOU KNOW WHAT SOMEONE IS THINKING.
ASK, "WHEN YOU SAID ..., DID YOU MEAN ...?"

YOU'RE LIKELY TO FIND YOURSELF IN THE SAME SITUATIONS OVER AND OVER UNTIL YOU FINALLY ADDRESS THE MESS INSIDE YOU AND CHANGE.

WHATEVER TRIAL YOU'RE IN RIGHT NOW, ASK GOD FOR A "COME UP HERE!"
MOMENT, WHERE HE RAISES YOU OUT OF THE MESS THAT'S UP IN YOUR FACE
AND SHOWS YOU HIS EAGLE-EYE VIEWPOINT OF ALL HE'S DOING IN THE MIDST.
USE THE GALATIANS 5:22-23 GAUGE AND LET HIM TRANSFORM YOU.

IF YOU HAVE BEEN IN AN INTIMATE RELATIONSHIP OUTSIDE OF MARRIAGE, OR HAD LUSTFUL THOUGHTS ABOUT A WOMAN, YOU HAVE BOUND YOURSELF "AS ONE" WITH HER. 1 CORINTHIANS 6:12-20, MATTHEW 5:27-28. TO REPENT AND CUT OFF THOSE UNHOLY TIES, YOU CAN PRAY SOMETHING LIKE THIS:

"LORD FORGIVE ME FOR _____ _____ . IN THE NAME OF JESUS, I BREAK ANY UNHOLY TIES TO _____(NAME), AND I BLESS HER (HIM) AND HER FUTURE MARRIAGE TO BE FOUNDED ON YOU, FOR YOU ALONE ARE TRUE LOVE. SET ME FREE FROM THE THOUGHT PROCESSES THAT LEAD ME IN WRONG DIRECTIONS, AND SET ME APART FOR THE ONE YOU HAVE CHOSEN FOR ME TO MARRY. TEACH ME HOW TO REMAIN PURE AND LED BY YOUR SPIRIT IN MY CHOICES AND THOUGHTS. HELP ME BE THE MAN OF GOD YOU CREATED ME TO BE AS A BROTH-ER TO MY SISTERS IN THE FAITH AND AS A HUSBAND TO THE WIFE YOU WILL BRING TO ME IN YOUR PERFECT TIMING...."

WHATEVER YOU HIDE IN SECRET THE ENEMY CAN USE AGAINST YOU.

SUBMIT TO YOUR LEADERS, BE A JOY NOT A BURDEN, PRAY FOR THEM,
RESPECT THEM, LOVE THEM, LIVE IN PEACE WITH THEM, AND HONOR THEM.

LET THE THINGS YOU DO EACH DAY TURN ALL EYES GOD'S WAY.

YOU'LL MAKE MISTAKES SOMETIMES. EVERYONE DOES. BUT EVEN YOUR SINS AND FLAWS CAN POINT PEOPLE TO THE LORD. IN FACT, SAYING, "I WAS WRONG; PLEASE FORGIVE ME" TO SOMEONE YOU'VE HURT SPARKLES WITH HIS GLORY. 1 JOHN 1.

DON'T BE AFRAID OF YOUR MISTAKES. MAKE THEM AN OPPORTUNITY TO BLESS OTHERS. PEOPLE DON'T LIKE IT WHEN YOU PRETEND YOU'RE PERFECT. THEY'D RATHER SEE YOU REAL: SHARING YOUR TROUBLES WITH THEM, ADMITTING WHEN YOU'RE WRONG, SERVING THE LORD BECAUSE IT COMES FROM YOUR HEART, NOT JUST TO PUT ON A SHOW.

WHAT ARE YOU AFRAID OF? ASK THE LORD AND WRITE IT ON THE LEFT.
THEN ASK HIM FOR THE WAYS HIS LOVE CASTS THAT FEAR OUT, HIS TRUTH
FOR YOUR LIES, 1 JOHN 4:18, AND WRITE IT ON THE RIGHT.

FEAR OF _____ _____

FEAR OF _____ _____

FEAR OF _____ _____

FEAR OF _____ _____

FEAR OF _____ _____

FEAR OF _____ _____

FEAR OF _____ _____

FEAR OF _____ _____

FEAR OF _____ _____

FEAR OF _____ _____

FEAR OF _____ _____

FEAR OF _____ _____

FEAR OF _____ _____

FEAR OF _____ _____

FEAR OF _____ _____

FEAR OF _____ _____

FEAR OF _____ _____

FEAR OF _____ _____

FEAR OF _____ _____

FEAR OF _____ _____

FEAR OF _____ _____

FEAR OF _____ _____

FEAR OF _____ _____

FEAR OF _____ _____

FEAR OF _____ _____

FEAR OF _____ _____

FEAR OF _____ _____

FEAR OF _____ _____

FEAR OF _____ _____

FEAR OF _____ _____

FEAR OF _____ _____

ASK THE LORD, "WHEN YOU LOOK AT ME, WHAT DO YOU SEE?" WRITE WHAT
HE SAYS TO YOUR HEART, AND RUN IT THROUGH THE THREE-FOLD SIEVE.

TO SEAL YOUR FREEDOM, DO A "WORD SEARCH." LOOK UP IN A
CONCORDANCE ALL THE VERSES THAT DEAL WITH YOUR ISSUE. FOR
EXAMPLE, IF YOU STRUGGLE WITH PRIDE, LOOK UP "PROUD," "HAUGHTY,"
"PRIDE," AND ALSO THE OPPOSITES OF "HUMILITY," "HUMBLE," "MEEK" AND
"LOWLY." WRITE WHAT GOD SAYS TO YOUR HEART HERE IN YOUR JOURNAL.

TO BUILD YOUR FAITH, TRY WRITING YOUR PRAYER REQUESTS ON THE LEFT
AND DATING THEM. THEN WHEN GOD ANSWERS, WRITE WHAT HE DID ON THE
RIGHT AND DATE IT.

BURNOUT HAPPENS WHEN YOU'RE DOING MORE THAN GOD'S ASKED YOU TO, OR YOU'RE DOING IT IN YOUR OWN STRENGTH.

HAND YOUR SCHEDULE TO GOD. ASK HIM TO SHOW YOU THE THINGS HE
WANTS YOU TO DO THIS SEASON. GALATIANS 1:10.

IS THERE ANYTHING YOU'RE DOING THAT GOD HASN'T ASKED YOU TO?

JUST BECAUSE YOU BELIEVE SOMETHING DOESN'T MEAN IT'S TRUE. ONLY WHAT
GOD SAYS IS TRUE. JOHN 8:42-47. LET GOD'S TRUTH BECOME YOURS.

IF YOU FEEL YOU CAN'T "HEAR" GOD YET, DON'T LET IT WORRY YOU. JUST
KEEP ASKING HIM QUESTIONS AND LOOKING FOR HIS ANSWERS. HE MAY NOT
ANSWER THE WAY YOU EXPECT, BUT IF YOU'RE SURRENDERED TO HIM,
HE WON'T LET YOU MISS HIS WILL.

Do you have any questions?
Or do yo want mentoring to help you grow in the Lord?
Write

MoreThanAConquerorBooks@gmail.com.

Follow Mikaela Vincent and More Than A Conqueror Books on
Twitter, Facebook, and Wordpress.

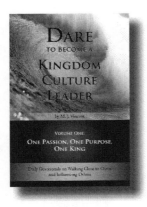 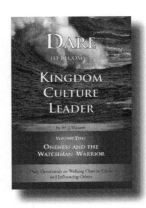

Consider the daily devotions in

Dare to Become a Kingdom Culture Leader
Volumes 1-2

to walk even deeper in the Lord and influence others to listen to
God's voice and follow His lead.

To order your copy today, visit
www.MoreThanAConquerorBooks.com

28082259R00070

Made in the USA
Columbia, SC
05 October 2018